To: _____

From: _____

Date: _____

Published by Christian Art Publishers
PO Box 1599, Vereeniging, 1930, RSA

© 2016
First edition 2016

Designed by Christian Art Publishers

Images used under license from Shutterstock.com

Printed in China

ISBN 978-1-4321-1596-8 CLR022

22 23 24 25 26 27 28 29 30 31 – 41 40 39 38 37 36 35 34 33 32

The Psalms in Color

COLORING BOOK

CHRISTIAN ART
PUBLISHERS

ENTER HIS
gates
WITH
Thanksgiving
&
HIS
COURTS
WITH
PRAISE
GIVE THANKS TO HIM
AND praise
HIS name
PSALM 100:4

As the
DEER
PANTS FOR STREAMS
OF WATER,
SO MY
SOUL
PANTS
FOR
YOU

MY
GOD

Psalm 42:1

Rest IN THE Lord, AND WAIT patiently FOR HIM.

PSALM 37:7

AS FOR ME, I WILL ALWAYS HAVE

HOPE

PSALM 71:14

PUT YOUR HOPE IN THE LORD. PSALM 37:34

GOD IS THE KING OF ALL THE EARTH; sing TO HIM A PSALM OF praise.

PSALM 47:7

How
precious
are Your
thoughts
about me.

When I wake up,
You are still with me!

PSALM 139:17-18

THE Truth OF THE LORD ENDURES forever.

PSALM 117:2

and know that I am God.

Psalm 46:10

Give THANKS to the Lord, for is GOOD! HE HIS faithful love endures forever.

⚘ Psalm 107:1 ⚘

When I am afraid,
I put my trust in You.

Psalm 56:3

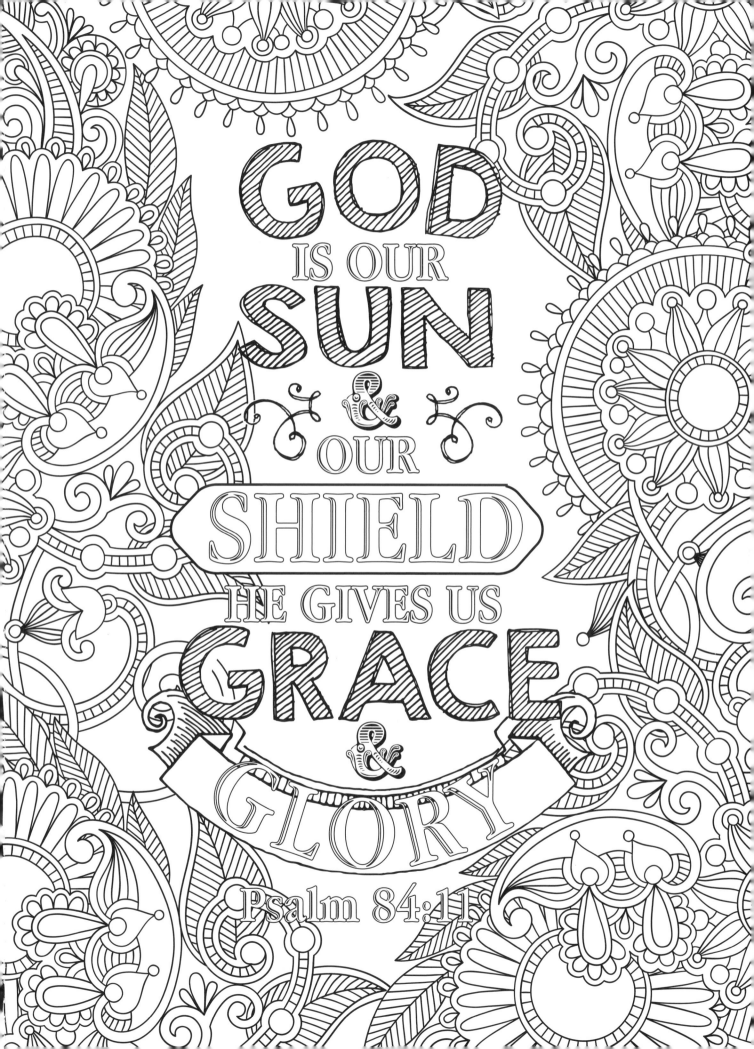

GOD IS OUR SUN & OUR SHIELD HE GIVES US GRACE & GLORY

Psalm 84:11

TRULY
MY SOUL
FINDS
REST
IN GOD.

PSALM 62:1

Whoever dwells in the shelter
of the Most High will rest
in the shadow of the Almighty.
Psalm 91:1

Psalm 61:2

From the ends of the earth I call to You, I call as my heart grows faint;
lead me to the rock that is higher than I.

My soul thirsts for God.

Psalm 42:2

JOY COMES IN THE MORNING

PSALM 30:5

CAST YOUR CARES ON THE
LORD
and He will sustain you.
PSALM 55:22

The LORD
is my strength
and my song.

Psalm 118:14

Shout for *joy* to the LORD, all the earth.

Worship the LORD with *gladness*;

come before Him with *joyful* songs.

Know that the LORD is God.

It is He who made us, and *we are His*;

we are His people, the sheep of His pasture.

Enter His gates with thanksgiving and His courts with praise;

give *thanks* to Him and praise His name.

For the LORD is good and His *love* endures forever;

His *faithfulness* continues through all generations.

Psalm 100

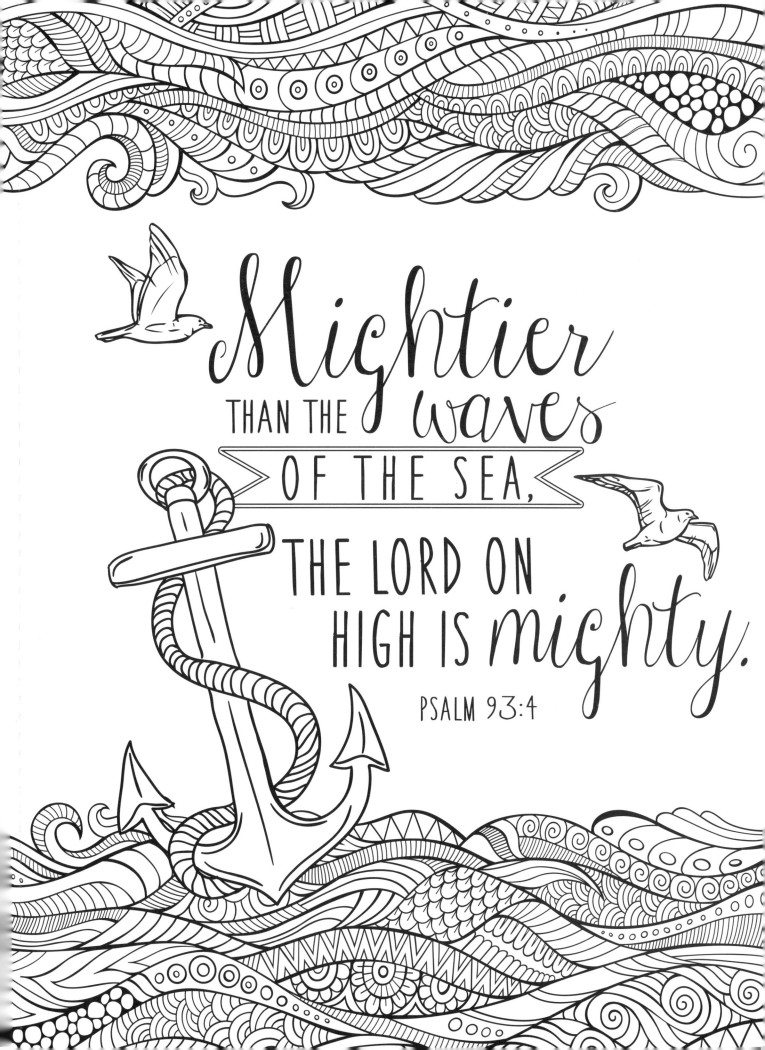

The LORD
is my shepherd;
I shall not want.
He makes me
lie down
in green pastures.
He leads me beside
still waters.
He restores my soul.
He leads me in paths
of righteousness
for His name's sake.
Even though I walk
through the valley of
the shadow of death,
I will fear no evil,
for You are with me;
Your rod and
Your staff,
they comfort me.
You prepare
a table before me
in the presence
of my enemies;
You anoint
my head with oil;
my cup overflows.
Surely goodness and
mercy shall follow me
all the days of my life,
and I shall dwell
in the house of
the LORD forever.

Psalm 23

Delight
YOURSELF IN THE
LORD
AND HE WILL GIVE YOU THE
DESIRES
OF YOUR

PSALM 37:4

Keep me as the *apple* of Your eye; hide me in the shadow of Your *wings.*

Psalm 17:8

Create
IN ME, A PURE
heart, O GOD,
AND RENEW A
steadfast
SPIRIT WITHIN ME.
~Psalm 51:10

Give *thanks*
to the LORD,
for He is good;
His *love* endures
forever.

Psalm 118:29

GREAT IS OUR LORD AND MIGHTY IN POWER.
PSALM 147:5

THE LORD, MY God, lights UP MY DARKNESS.

PSALM 18:28

Great is the LORD! Psalm 35:27

I lift up my eyes
to the mountains –
where does my help come from?
My help comes from the LORD,
the Maker of heaven
and earth.

PSALM 121:1-2

He will cover you
WITH HIS FEATHERS,
And under His wings
YOU WILL FIND REFUGE.

⤙ PSALM 91:4 ⤚

I prayed to the LORD,
and He answered me.

Psalm 34:4

Shout for **joy**
to the LORD,
all the **earth**.

Psalm 98:4

HAPPY

ARE THE PEOPLE WHOSE
GOD IS THE LORD!

PSALM 144:15

HE SHALL GIVE
His angels CHARGE OVER YOU *to keep you* IN ALL YOUR WAYS.

PSALM 91:11

As far as the east is from the west,
so far has He removed our transgressions from us.

Psalm 103:12

*I know that the LORD is great,
and that our Lord is above all gods.*

Psalm 135:5

The LORD is merciful & filled with unfailing LOVE

Psalm 103:8

THE LORD
BLESSES HIS PEOPLE WITH PEACE.
PSALM 29:11

God arms me with strength,

and He makes my way perfect. Psalm 18:32

The
LORD
HAS DONE
great things
FOR US
AND WE ARE FILLED WITH
joy.
PSALM 126:3

PSALM 8:1

O LORD, HOW

MAJESTIC

IS YOUR NAME IN ALL
THE EARTH!

God is our *refuge* and *Strength.* Psalm 46:1

Trust IN THE LORD. Psalm 4:5

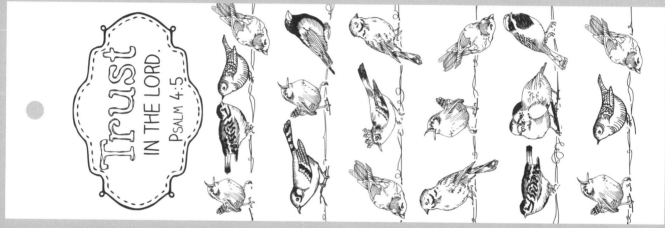

Pray more worry less

REJOICE IN THE LORD AND BE GLAD. Psalm 32:11

FOLD HERE

May you be blessed
by the Lord, the Maker
of heaven and earth.
PSALM 115:15

Give thanks to the LORD,
for He is good;
His love endures forever.

PSALM 118:29

FOLD HERE

May He give you the desire
of your heart and make all
your plans succeed.

PSALM 20:4

God is good.

May God bless you.

Sing for joy!

Where God guides, He provides.

Where the will of God leads you, the grace of God will keep you.

Rejoice in the Lord!

God loves you!

GIFT TAGS
Color, cut, punch, tie a ribbon
and write your own special message.

HAVE A *blessed day!*

You are precious & loved

Sing a SONG OF *praise!*

GIFT TAGS
Color, cut, punch, tie a ribbon
and write your own special message.